Basic Snare Drum

by

Steve Faulkner

Photo by Shullamuth

STEVE FAULKNER is a career musician and private drum instructor. He has toured the USA and Europe with various bands. He is currently playing and recording with Secret City Band. Secret City Band has two CD's out, Secret City (2017) and Touch the Sky (2022). Steve was the drum instructor with Rockley Music in Lakewood, CO until they closed their doors in December 2019. He currently is in the Dixon Signature Program with Dixon Drums, Artist Support Program with London Drumsticks, and is an endorser with Saluda Cymbals. Steve has recorded with various bands.

Steve Faulkner
stevecdrum@aol.com

Table of Contents

Foreword

A beginning snare drum method should provide fundamentals and basic theory for the student. This information is vital to playing the instrument well. That basic information is as follows: how to hold the sticks and strike the drum properly, what time signatures mean, recognizing what different notes and rests look like, how much value they receive and how they are counted. You must also learn how to interpret your expression marks (loud and soft places in the music). All of this information is covered in this book. With this basic theory, you will develop you reading skills, equal use of both hands, hand speed, as well as your rhythmic and musical ideas.

This is a step by step method that starts on the ground floor, and progresses in difficulty. By learning step by step, you will be able to play the beginning rhythm patterns that progress into more intricate rhythm.

Upon completion of this book, you will have a strong foundation in snare drumming that will allow you to play advanced material.

Introductory Page
and Explanations

Every piece of music has a time signature.

4/4 time means - 4 beats in a measure and a quarter note gets 1 beat.

2/4 time means - 2 beats in a measure and a quarter note gets 1 beat.

The top number in any time signature tells you how many beats there will be in a measure.

The bottom number in the time signature tells you what kind of a note will receive 1 beat.

If a 4 is on the bottom, the quarter note will receive 1 beat.

If you do not know which note receives 1 beat, you can not determine the values of the other notes and rests.

Following are the values of the other notes and rests, and what they look like.

Please learn the name of the notes and rests, what they look like, and how they are written.

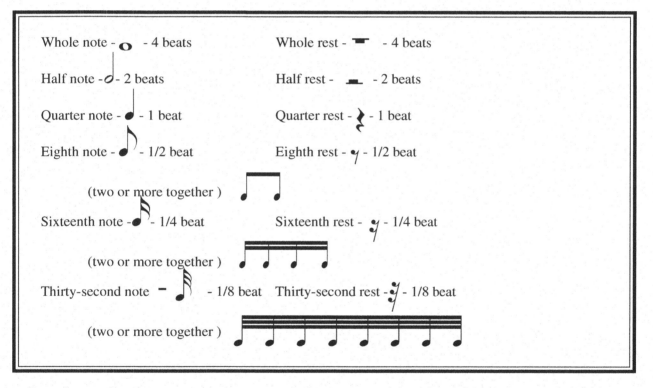

In order to play these notes and rests properly, you must know how they are counted. This will be explained in detail in the following pages of the book. Also, please be aware of what a measure is. *A measure is what is written between the barlines.* A barline is the vertical line that separates the measures. If we are playing in 4/4 time, the measure must have 4 beats in it. These 4 beats can be any combination of notes and rests, providing the value does not exceed 4 beats. If we are playing in 2/4 time, each measure must contain 2 beats. Once again, these 2 beats can be any combination of notes and rests providing the value does not exceed 2 beats.

How To Hold The Sticks

Matched grip. Put the stick between thumb and index finger. Wrap your other fingers around the stick. Bring the stick under your wrist. On the up stroke, allow your fingers to let the stick come away from the palm of the hand. On the down stroke, let the fingers and wrist come down together. Do not squeeze the stick. Play with a loose relaxed grip. Both hands work this way in the matched grip.

Traditional grip. Right hand is the same as in the matched grip. There is more than one technique for the left hand. We are going to discuss one of the more common ways to use the left hand. Put your hand out straight, palm up. Put the stick between your hand and thumb. Put your index finger over the stick. Put your middle finger on the outside of the stick. If you put the middle finger over the stick, you hurt the mobility of the stick. Your ring finger and little finger should go under the stick. Put your thumb on the index finger. This will release the pressure between the thumb and hand. Tilt the wrist downward. Your left wrist will work in a sideways motion, while the right wrist will work straight up and down. Do not turn the left wrist into the body. Do not squeeze the stick. Play with a loose relaxed grip. It is important to know that either grip is right. Use whichever grip feels best to you. Play with good habits and technique. If you don't, you will make easy rhythms harder to play, and harder rhythms impossible to play.

Directions for Text

Matched grip

Example 1   Pat your foot on all 4 beats. Repeat each line one time.

Line 1:   These are whole notes worth 4 beats each. Strike the whole note on beat 1, and pat your foot on all four beats. You hold the whole note 4 beats, but you strike the note just one time. Alternate each note, and repeat the line one time.

Line 2:   There is a whole note in the first measure, followed by a whole rest in the 2nd measure. This pattern is the same for measures 3 and 4. Count the whole rest 1,2,3, 4. The whole note and rest each get 4 beats.

Line 3:   The line has whole notes in the first 3 measures, and a whole rest in the 4th measure.

Line 4:   Measures 1 and 2 have whole notes in them. The 3rd measure is a whole rest. The 4th measure is a whole note.

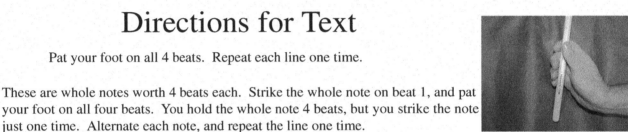

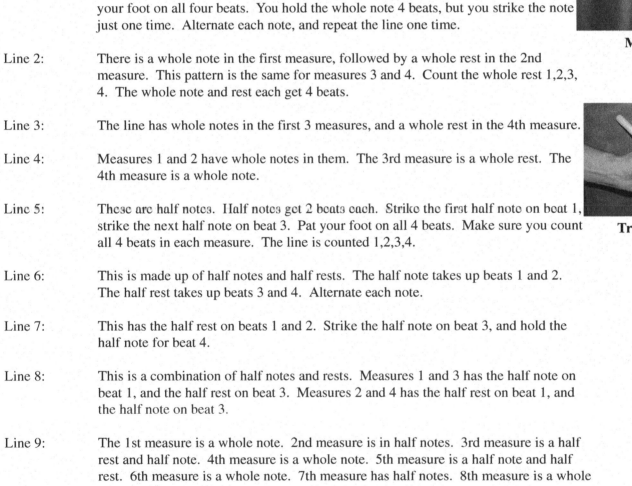

Traditional grip

Line 5:   These are half notes. Half notes get 2 beats each. Strike the first half note on beat 1, strike the next half note on beat 3. Pat your foot on all 4 beats. Make sure you count all 4 beats in each measure. The line is counted 1,2,3,4.

Line 6:   This is made up of half notes and half rests. The half note takes up beats 1 and 2. The half rest takes up beats 3 and 4. Alternate each note.

Line 7:   This has the half rest on beats 1 and 2. Strike the half note on beat 3, and hold the half note for beat 4.

Line 8:   This is a combination of half notes and rests. Measures 1 and 3 has the half note on beat 1, and the half rest on beat 3. Measures 2 and 4 has the half rest on beat 1, and the half note on beat 3.

Line 9:   The 1st measure is a whole note. 2nd measure is in half notes. 3rd measure is a half rest and half note. 4th measure is a whole note. 5th measure is a half note and half rest. 6th measure is a whole note. 7th measure has half notes. 8th measure is a whole note. Repeat to the beginning and play both lines one more time.

NOTES:

Example 1

Repeat Sign- Repeat to the beginning and play line one more time.

Alternate each note.

Repeat to the beginning and play both lines again.

7

Example 2

Line 1: These are quarter notes worth 1 beat each. The line is counted 1,2,3,4. Pat your foot on all 4 beats, and alternate each quarter note. Strike one quarter note for each beat.

Line 2: This has quarter notes and quarter rests in each measure. In the 1st measure the quarter rest is on beat 4. 2nd measure the rest is on beat 4. 3rd measure the rest is on beat 3. 4th measure the rest is on beat 3. Alternate each note even though you have a quarter rest separating the notes.

Line 3: This is written in quarter notes and quarter rests. In the first 2 measures the quarter rest is on beat 2. In measures 3 and 4 the quarter rest is on beat 1.

Line 4: This has the quarter rest on beat 4 in the 1st and 3rd measures, beat 1 in the 2nd and 4th measures.

Line 5: This has the quarter rest on beats 2 and 3 in the first two measures, beats 1 and 4 in measures 3 and 4.

Line 6: This has the quarter rest on beats 3 and 4 in the 1st, 3rd, and 4th measures. In the 2nd measure the quarter rest is on beats 1 and 2.

NOTES:

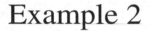

Example 3

Line 7: This has the quarter rest on beats 2 and 4 in the first two measures, and on beats 1 and 3 in the last two measures.

Line 8: This has the quarter rest on beats 1 and 3 in the 1st and 4th measures, and on beats 2 and 4 in the 2nd and 3rd measures.

Line 9: This is written in quarter notes and quarter rests. This is 12 measures long. Please notice that the piece ends right handed. On the repeat, start the piece with your left hand. Pat your foot on all 4 beats in every measure.

Line 10: This is 16 measures long. The piece ends right handed, so on the repeat, start the piece left handed. Alternate each note and pat your foor on all 4 beats in every measure.

NOTES:

Example 3

9

Example 4

Line 1: Line 1 is comprised of eighth notes and quarter notes. The eighth notes receive 1/2 a beat each. The first two measures are counted 1& 2& 3& 4&. Put your foot down on 1, up on &, down on 2, up on &, down on 3, up on &, down on 4, up on &.When the foot makes the down and up stroke, you have patted one full beat. Therefore, when the foot goes down, that is half a beat. When the foot comes up, that is the other half of the beat. Let's count the whole line. The counting goes like this:

 1& 2& 3& 4&. 1& 2& 3& 4&. 1& 2 3 4. 1& 2 3 4.

Line 2: This is counted 1& 2& 3 4. 1& 2& 3 4. 1 2 3& 4&. 1 2 3& 4&.

Line 3: This is counted 1 2& 3& 4. 1 2& 3& 4. 1& 2 3 4&. 1& 2 3 4&.

Line 4: This is counted 1 2 3& 4. 1 2, 3& 4. 1 2& 3 4&. 1 2& 3 4&.

Line 5: This is counted 1 2& 3 4. 1 2& 3 4. 1 2 3 4&. 1 2 3 4&.

Line 6: This is counted 1& 2 3 4. 1 2& 3 4. 1 2 3& 4. 1 2 3 4&.

Line 7: This is counted 1& 2& 3 4. 1 2 3& 4&. 1 2& 3& 4. 1& 2 3 4&.

Line 8: This is counted 1& 2 3& 4&. 1 2& 3& 4. 1& 2 3& 4. 1& 2& 3 4.

Line 9: This is 12 measures long. This piece starts right handed, and ends left handed. So, when you repeat the piece, you will start with your right hand. Make sure that when you say the "&" of the beat, your foot is up. Lets count each measure. The counting goes like this:

 1& 2& 3& 4&. 1 2& 3& 4. 1 2& 3 4&. 1 2 3& 4&.
 1& 2 3 4&. 1& 2 3 4. 1& 2& 3 4. 1 2 3& 4.
 1& 2 3& 4. 1& 2& 3& 4&. 1 2& 3& 4. 1& 2& 3 4.

NOTES:

Example 4

11

Example 5

Line 10:   Line 10 is 16 measures long. This piece starts right handed, and ends right handed. Therefore, on the repeat, start the piece with your left hand. The counting goes like this:

1 2& 3& 4&.   1& 2& 3 4&.   1& 2 3& 4&.   1& 2& 3& 4.
1 2& 3& 4.   1& 2& 3 4.   1& 2 3& 4.   1 2 3& 4&.
1& 2 3 4&.   1& 2& 3& 4&.   1 2& 3 4&.   1 2 3& 4.
1& 2& 3 4.   1 2& 3& 4.   1& 2 3& 4&.   1 2& 3 4.

Line 1:   This 12 measure piece is comprised of quarter notes, quarter rests, and eighth notes. This starts with your right hand, and ends with your right hand. When you repeat, start left handed. The counting goes like this:

1& 2 3 4&.   1 2& 3& 4&.   1 2 3& 4.   1& 2& 3 4.
1 2 3& 4&.   1 2& 3 4&.   1 2 3& 4.   1 2& 3& 4.
1 2& 3 4&.   1& 2 3 4.   1 2& 3& 4.   1& 2 3& 4.

NOTES:

Example 5

12

Example 6

Line 2:   This is 16 measures long. This is comprised of quarter notes, quarter rests, and eighth notes. The piece will begin with your right hand both times. The counting goes like this:

1 2 3 4&. 1& 2& 3 4. 1 2 3& 4&. 1 2 3& 4.
1 2& 3& 4. 1 2& 3 4&. 1& 2& 3 4&. 1 2& 3 4.
1& 2& 3 4&. 1& 2 3& 4&. 1 2& 3 4&. 1& 2& 3 4.
1 2 3& 4&. 1& 2 3 4&. 1 2 3& 4&. 1 2& 3& 4.

Line 3:   This is 16 measures long. Since the piece ends right handed, start with your left hand on the repeat. The counting goes like this:

1 2 3& 4. 1& 2& 3 4&. 1 2 3& 4&. 1 2& 3& 4.
1& 2 3& 4. 1 2& 3& 4. 1& 2 3 4&. 1 2 3& 4&.
1& 2& 3 4. 1 2 3& 4&. 1 2& 3& 4. 1 2& 3 4&.
1 2& 3& 4. 1 2 3& 4&. 1& 2 3 4&. 1 2& 3& 4.

NOTES:

Example 6

13

Example 7

Lines 1-8 are comprised of eighth notes and eighth rests. The eighth rest gets 1/2 beat (just like the eighth note). Since these are written in eighth notes and rests, all of the lines are counted 1& 2& 3& 4&. Lets take a look at where the eighth rest is written in each measure of each line.

Line 1:   The eighth rest is on beat 1 in the 1st and 2nd measures, and on the & of 1 in the 3rd and 4th measures.

Line 2:   The eighth rest is on beat 2 in the first two measures, and on the & of 2 in the last two measures.

Line 3:   The eighth rest is on beat 3 in the first two measures, and on the & of 3 in the last two measures.

Line 4:   The eighth rest is on beat 4 in the first two measures, and on the & of 4 in the last two measures.

Line 5:   The eighth rest is on beats 1 and 2 in the first two measures, and on beats 3 and 4 in the last two measures.

Line 6:   The eighth rest is on beats 2 and 4 in the first two measures, and on beats 1 and 3 in the last two measures.

Line 7:   The eighth rest is on beats 1 and 4 in the first two measures, and on beats 2 and 3 in the last two measures.

Line 8:   The eighth rest is on the & of 1, beat 2, the & of 3, beat 4 in the first two measures. In the 3rd and 4th measures the eighth rest is on beat 1, & of 2, beat 3, & of 4.

Line 9:   This is 12 measures long. The piece will begin with your right hand both times. Make sure that your foot is up on the & of each beat.

NOTES:

14

Example 7

12 measures

15

Example 8

Line 10:   This is 16 measures long. Since the piece ends with your right hand, start with your left hand on the repeat.

Line 11:   This is 16 measures long and begins with your right hand each time.

NOTES:

Example 8

16 measures

16 measures

Example 9

Line 1: This is comprised of quarter notes, quarter rests (1 beat each), eighth notes, and eighth rests (1/2 beat each). This piece is 16 measures long. Count whole beats for quarter notes and quarter rests (1,2,3,4), and half beats for eighth notes and eighth rests (1& 2& 3& 4&). The counting goes like this:

1& 2 3& 4. 1& 2 3& 4&. 1& 2 3& 4&. 1 2& 3& 4&.
1& 2& 3& 4&. 1 2& 3& 4. 1& 2& 3 4&. 1 2& 3& 4&.
1& 2& 3& 4. 1 2 3& 4&. 1& 2& 3& 4&. 1& 2 3 4&.
1& 2& 3& 4&. 1& 2& 3 4&. 1& 2 3& 4&. 1& 2& 3& 4&.

Line 2: This is comprised of quarter notes, quarter rests, eighth notes, and eighth rests. This piece is 16 measures long. Since the piece ends right handed, start with your left hand on the repeat. The counting goes like this:

1 2& 3& 4&. 1& 2 3 4&. 1 2& 3& 4&. 1& 2& 3& 4&.
1& 2& 3 4. 1& 2 3& 4&. 1& 2& 3& 4&. 1 2& 3& 4&.
1& 2& 3 4&. 1 2& 3& 4&. 1& 2& 3& 4&. 1& 2& 3 4&.
1& 2 3& 4&. 1& 2& 3& 4&. 1 2 3& 4&. 1 2& 3& 4&.

NOTES:

Example 9

17

Example 10

Lines 1-8 are combinations of sixteenth notes and sixteenth rests. Sixteenth notes and rests receive 1/4 beat each. They are counted 1e&ah 2e&ah. Your foot goes down on 1, and comes up on the "&" of the beat. Put your foot back down on 2, bring your foot up on the & of the beat. Do not bring the foot up on the "e" of the beat. Do not put your foot down on the "ah" of the beat. The reasoning behind this is to keep steady time with your foot. The foot should be down for 1/2 a beat (1e), and up for 1/2 a beat (&ah). Please notice that this is written in 2/4 time. This means that there is 2 beats in a measure, a quarter note gets 1 beat.

Line 1: These are sixteenth notes without any sixteenth rests written in between them. This means that you play a note for every 1/4 beat that you count. Count the line 1e&ah, 2e&ah.

Line 2: Here is a new subject. The new subject is a repeat measure. A repeat measure is an easy way to write the same measure one more time. Be aware of the sixteenth rest in each measure. In the first two measures the sixteenth rest is on beat 1 and beat 2. In measures 3 and 4, the sixteenth rest is on the e of 1, and the e of 2.

Line 3: The sixteenth rest is on the & of 1, and the & of 2 in the first two measures. The sixteenth rest is on the ah of 1, and the ah of 2 in the last two measures.

Line 4: Rest on beat 1 and beat 2 in the first two measures. Rest on the & of 1, and the & of 2 in the last two measures.

Line 5: Rest on the ah of 1 and the ah of 2 in the first two measures. Rest on the e of 1 and the e of 2 in the 2nd and 4th measures.

Line 6: Rest on the & of 1 and the & of 2 in the 1st and 3rd measures. Rest on the e of 1 and the e of 2 in the 2nd and 4th measures.

Line 7: Rest on the ah of 1 and the ah of 2 in the 1st and 3rd measures. Rest on the e of 1 and the e of 2 in the 2nd and 4th measures.

Line 8: Rest on the & of 1 and the & of 2 in the 1st and 3rd measures. Rest on beat 1 and 2 in the 2nd and 4th measures.

Line 9: This is 12 measures long. It is comprised of different combinations of sixteenth notes and sixteenth rests. Let's take a look at where the sixteenth rest is written in each measure.

      1st measure -   rest on the ah of 1 and the ah of 2.
      2nd measure -   beat 1 and beat 2.
      3rd measure -   e of 1, e of 2.
      4th measure -   & of 1, & of 2.
      5th measure -   beat 1, ah of 1. Beat 2, ah of 2.
      6th measure -   e of 1, & of 1. e of 2, & of 2.
      7th measure -   e of 1, beat 2.
      8th measure -   beat 1, e of 2.
      9th measure -   & of 1, ah of 2.
      10th measure -   beat 1, e of 2.
      11th measure -   & of 1, ah of 2
      12th measure -   ah of 1, beat 2.

Since line 9 ends left handed, the piece starts right handed on the repeat. Make sure to alternate each note.

NOTES:

Example 10

* Repeat measure- Repeat measure you just played one more time.

Example 11

Line 10:   Line 10 is 16 measures long. The last note in the last measure is right handed. When you repeat, start with your left hand. Let's take a look at where the sixteenth rest is written in each measure.

1st measure-	all sixteenth notes.
2nd measure-	beat 1, e of 2.
3rd measure-	& of 1, ah of 2.
4th measure-	ah of 1, e of 2.
5th measure-	& of 1, the e and the & of 2.
6th measure-	beat 1and the ah of 1, beat 2.
7th measure-	ah of 1, e of 2.
8th measure-	& of 1. Beat 2, ah of 2.
9th measure-	beat 1, ah of 2.
10th measure-	& of 1, & of 2.
11th measure-	ah of 1, e of 2.
12th measure-	beat 1, & of 2.
13th measure-	e of 1, beat 2.
14th measure-	& of 1, e of 2.
15th measure-	ah of 1, beat 2.
16th measure-	e of 2, ah of 2.

Line 11:   This is 16 measures long. This ends right handed, so on the repeat, start with your left hand. Let's take a look at where the sixteenth rest is written in each measure.

1st measure-	beat 1and the & of 1. Beat 2 and the & of 2.
2nd measure-	e and the ah of 1, e and the ah of 2
3rd measure-	e of 1, & of 2.
4th measure-	e and the & of 1. Beat 2 and the & of 2.
5th measure-	ah of 1. Beat 2 and the ah of 2.
6th measure-	& of 1, ah of 2.
7th measure-	beat 1, ah of 1. Beat 2, ah of 2.
8th measure-	e of 1, & of 1, e of 2, & of 2.
9th measure-	beat 1, ah of 1, e of 2, & of 2.
10th measure-	& of 1, & of 2.
11th measure-	e of 1, e of 2.
12th measure-	beat 1, & of 2.
13th measure-	beat 1, ah of 1, ah of 2.
14th measure-	e of 1, e of 2, & of 2.
15th measure-	beat 1, beat 2, ah of 2.
16th measure-	& of 1, e of 2, ah of 2.

NOTES:

Example 11

Example 12

Line 1: This is 16 measures long. This is a combination of eighth note and sixteenth note rhythms. Let's talk about how this is counted and why it is counted that way. For example, the first measure is counted- 1 &ah, 2e&. When you count this, you are not just pulling syllables out of mid-air. What you are counting is the value of the notes. An eighth note and two sixteenths is counted 1 &ah because of the value of each note. 1 &ah is a note worth 1/2 beat, followed by two notes that are worth 1/4 beat each. 1 &ah (1/2, 1/4, 1/4). When you count 2e&, you are counting 1/4, 1/4, 1/2 (two sixteenths and an eighth). So, 1 &ah, 2e& in value is 1/2, 1/4, 1/4, 1/4, 1/4, 1/2. Here is a measure by measure break down of how this piece is counted. Alternate each note, and the piece will start right handed both times.

> 1 &ah 2e&. 1e& 2 &ah. 1 &ah 2&ah. 1e& 2e&.
> 1e&ah 2 &ah. 1e& 2e&ah. 1 &ah 2e&. 1e&ah 2 &.
> 1e&ah 2e&. 1e& 2 &ah. 1 & 2e&ah. 1e& 2 &.
> 1e&ah 2e&ah. 1 &ah 2e&ah. 1e&ah 2 &. 1e&ah 2.

Line 2: This is 16 measures long. This combines eighth notes, eighth rests, and sixteenth notes. Since the piece ends right handed, start with your left hand on the repeat. Here is how the piece is counted.

> 1 & 2e&. 1 & 2 &ah. 1e&ah 2 &. 1 & 2e&.
> 1 &ah 2e&ah. 1e& 2 &. 1 &ah 2 &ah. 1e& 2.
> 1e&ah 2 &ah. 1e& 2e&ah. 1 &ah 2 &ah. 1e& 2 &ah.
> 1 &ah 2 &ah. 1 &ah 2e&. 1e&ah 2 &. 1 & 2e&.

NOTES:

Example 12

23

Example 13

Line 3: This is 16 measures long, and starts right handed both times through. This is a combination of eighth notes, eighth rests, and sixteenth notes. Here is how the piece is counted.

    1e& 2e&. 1 &ah 2 &ah. 1 &ah 2e&. 1e& 2 &ah.
    1e&ah 2 &ah. 1 &ah 2e&ah. 1e& 2e&ah. 1e&ah 2 &.
    1 & 2e&. 1 &ah 2 &ah. 1e& 2 &. 1 & 2e&.
    1 &ah 2e&. 1e& 2 &ah. 1 &ah 2e&. 1e&ah 2 &.

Line 4: This is 16 measures long, and starts right handed both times through. This is a combination of eighth notes, eighth rests, and sixteenth notes. Here is how the piece is counted.

    1e& 2 &ah. 1 &ah 2 &. 1e& 2 &. 1 &ah 2e&.
    1e& 2 &ah. 1 &ah 2 &. 1e&ah 2 &. 1 &ah 2e&.
    1 & 2e&. 1 & 2 &ah. 1 & 2e&ah. 1e& 2 &ah.
    1e& 2 &ah. 1e& 2 &. 1 &ah 2e&ah. 1e&ah 2e&.

NOTES:

Example 13

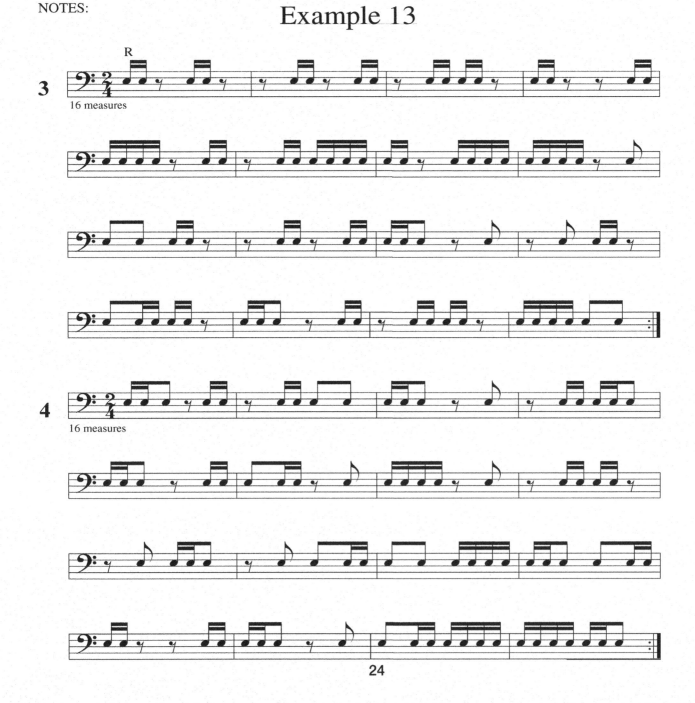

24

Example 14

Line 5: This is 16 measures long, and combines sixteenth notes, sixteenth rests, eighth notes, and eighth rests. In order to play this in good steady time, I suggest you count out every 1/4 beat for the sixteenth notes and sixteenth rests. Make sure your foot goes down on the beat (the 1 or the 2), and comes up on the & of the beat. This way your foot is even in the time you keep. The foot will be down for 1/2 beat, and up for 1/2 beat. Since the piece ends right handed, start with your left hand when you repeat. Here is how the piece is counted.

> 1e&ah 2 &. 1e&ah 2e&ah. 1 & 2e&. 1 &ah 2.
> 1e& 2e&. 1 &ah 2e&ah. 1e& 2 &ah. 1e&ah 2 &.
> 1e&ah 2 &ah. 1e& 2e&ah. 1e&ah 2 &ah. 1e&ah 2 &.
> 1 &ah 2e&ah. 1e& 2 &. 1 & 2 &ah. 1 &ah 2e&.

Line 6:   1 &ah 2e&ah. 1e ah 2 &ah. 1 &ah 2 &. 1e&ah 2e&.
> 1e&ah 2 &ah 1e& 2e&. 1 &ah 2e ah. 1e&ah 2 &.
> 1 &ah 2e&ah 1e&ah 2 &. 1 & 2e ah. 1e& 2 &.
> 1e ah 2e&ah. 1e&ah 2 &. 1 &ah 2 &ah. 1e&ah 2.

* Please be aware that the sixteenth - eighth - sixteenth note phrase will be played the same as two sixteenth notes, a sixteenth rest, and a sixteenth note.

NOTES:

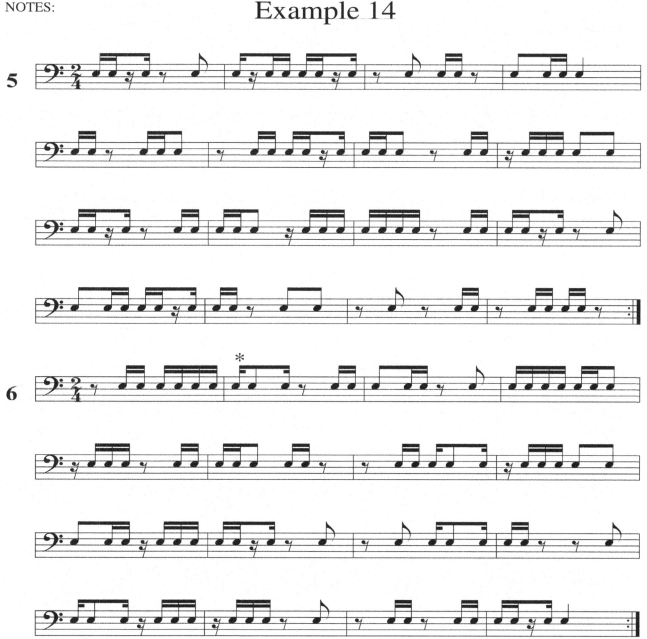

25

Example 15

New subject. These are **triplets**. In order to play a triplet, you must know the definition of a triplet. *A triplet is 3 notes played in the value of 2 notes*. If you add the value of 2 of the notes, you have the value of the triplet. We can have half note triplets, quarter note triplets, eighth note triplets, sixteenth note triplets. In this case we are starting with eighth note triplets. I think the eighth note triplet is the easiest triplet to start with since the triplet will receive 1 beat. Since eighth notes are worth 1/2 beat in 4/4 time, you add two eighth notes together, 1/2+1/2, and you get 1 beat. Hence the definition, 3 notes played in the value of 2 notes.

Now, how do you count these triplets? Count the beat the triplet begins on, followed by the word triplet. For instance, line 1 is written in eighth note triplets. The counting for the line will be 1triplet, 2triplet, 3triplet, 4triplet. Pat your foot on the beginning of each triplet (your foot pats on 1,2,3,4). The foot comes up between the 2nd and 3rd note of the triplet. Sometimes this is a little hard to feel at first. If this is true for you, let me give you a suggestion. Put your foot down on the 1st note of the triplet, and bring your foot up on the 3rd note of the triplet. This is not exactly even time, but it will allow you to begin to play the phrase smoothly. Once you have done this, try to pat the foot in the way I first described. Please realize that straight eighth note triplets will be started hand to hand. Beat one will be right handed, beat 2 will start left handed, beat 3 right handed, beat 4 left handed. These lines combine eighth note triplets and quarter notes.

Here is how these lines are counted. Alternate each note.

Line 1: 1triplet 2triplet 3triplet 4triplet. (All 4 measures counted this way).

Line 2: Measures 1 and 2 counted - 1 2triplet 3triplet 4triplet. Measures 3 and 4 counted - 1triplet 2 3triplet 4triplet.

Line 3: Measures 1 and 2 counted - 1triplet 2triplet 3 4triplet. Measures 3 and 4 counted - 1triplet 2triplet 3triplet 4.

Line 4: Measures 1 and 2 counted - 1 2triplet 3triplet 4. Measures 3 and 4 counted - 1triplet 2 3 4triplet.

Line 5: Measures 1 and 2 counted - 1triplet 2triplet 3 4. Measures 3 and 4 counted - 1 2 3triplet 4triplet.

Line 6: Measures 1 and 2 counted - 1triplet 2 3triplet 4. Measures 3 and 4 counted - 1 2triplet 3 4triplet.

Line 7: Measures 1 and 2 counted - 1 2triplet 3triplet 4triplet. Measures 3 and 4 counted - 1triplet 2triplet 3triplet 4.

Line 8: This is counted - 1 2triplet 3triplet 4triplet. 1triplet 2 3triplet 4triplet. 1triplet 2triplet 3 4triplet. 1triplet 2triplet 3triplet 4.

Line 9: This is 12 measures long. The piece will begin right handed both times through. Here is how the piece is counted:

> 1 2triplet 3 4triplet. 1triplet 2 3triplet 4. 1triplet 2triplet 3 4. 1 2 3triplet 4triplet.
> 1triplet 2 3 4triplet. 1 2triplet 3triplet 4. 1 2triplet 3 4. 1triplet 2 3triplet 4triplet.
> 1triplet 2triplet 3 4. 1 2triplet 3triplet 4triplet. 1triplet 2 3triplet 4triplet. 1triplet 2triplet 3 4.

NOTES:

Example 15

Example 16

Line 1: This is a combination of eighth notes (1/2 beat each) and eighth note triplets (1 beat each). This piece is 12 measures long. If you alternate each note, the piece ends right handed. When you repeat, begin with your left hand. Here is how the piece is counted:

1 & 2triplet 3triplet 4 &. 1 & 2triplet 3 & 4triplet. 1triplet 2 & 3 & 4triplet.
1 & 2 & 3triplet 4triplet. 1triplet 2triplet 3 & 4 &. 1triplet 2 & 3triplet 4 &.
1 & 2triplet 3triplet 4triplet. 1triplet 2triplet 3triplet 4 &. 1triplet 2 & 3triplet 4triplet.
1triplet 2triplet 3 & 4triplet. 1 & 2triplet 3triplet 4 &. 1triplet 2triplet 3triplet 4 &.

Line 2: This is 12 measures long. This piece combines eighth notes, eighth rests, and eighth note triplets. Look the piece over before you play it. Realize where the eighth rest falls in each measure. Here is how the piece is counted.

1triplet 2 & 3triplet 4 &. 1triplet 2 & 3 & 4triplet. 1 & 2triplet 3 & 4triplet.
1 & 2triplet 3triplet 4 &. 1 & 2 & 3triplet 4triplet. 1triplet 2triplet 3 & 4 &.
1triplet 2triplet 3triplet 4 &. 1triplet 2triplet 3 & 4triplet. 1triplet 2 & 3triplet 4triplet.
1 & 2triplet 3triplet 4triplet. 1triplet 2triplet 3 & 4triplet. 1 & 2triplet 3triplet 4 &.

NOTES:

Example 16

29

Example 17

Line 3: This is 12 measures long and combines eighth notes, eighth rests, and eighth note triplets. By now, you know to count the eighth notes and rests in syllables of half beats (1 & 2 & 3 & 4 &). You also know to count the eighth note triplets in whole beats (1triplet 2triplet 3triplet 4triplet). With this in mind, let's take a look at where the eighth rest is written in each measure.

          1st measure -   no eighth rests.
          2nd measure -   rest on 2 and 3.
          3rd measure -   rest on 4.
          4th measure -   rest on 1.
          5th measure -   rest on 3.
          6th measure -   rest on 2.
          7th measure -   rest on 1 and 4.
          8th measure -   rest on 3 and 4.
          9th measure -   rest on 3.
          10th measure - rest on 2.
          11th measure - rest on 4.
          12th measure - rest on 3.

Line 4: This is 12 measures long and combines eighth notes, eighth rests, and eighth note triplets. Since this piece ends right handed, start with your left hand when you repeat. Let's take a look at where the eighth rest is written in each measure.

          1st measure -   rest on 1 and 2.
          2nd measure -   rest on 4.
          3rd measure -   rest on 2 and 4.
          4th measure -   rest on 4.
          5th measure -   rest on 2.
          6th measure -   rest on 2 and 4.
          7th measure -   rest on 3.
          8th measure -   rest on 2 and 3.
          9th measure -   rest on 3.
          10th measure - rest on 1 and 4.
          11th measure - rest on 4.
          12th measure - rest on 2 and 4.

NOTES:

Example 17

Example 18

Line 5: This is 12 measures long and combines sixteenth notes (1/4 beat each), and eighth note triplets (1 beat each). Here is how this piece is counted.

1e&ah 2triplet 3triplet 4e&ah. 1triplet 2e&ah 3e&ah 4triplet. 1e&ah 2e&ah 3triplet 4triplet.
1e&ah 2triplet 3e&ah 4triplet. 1triplet 2triplet 3e&ah 4e&ah. 1triplet 2e&ah 3triplet 4e&ah.
1e&ah 2triplet 3triplet 4triplet. 1triplet 2triplet 3e&ah 4triplet. 1triplet 2e&ah 3triplet 4e&ah.
1triplet 2e&ah 3triplet 4triplet. 1triplet 2e&ah 3e&ah 4triplet. 1e&ah 2triplet 3triplet 4e&ah.

Line 6: This is 12 measures long and combines eighth notes, sixteenth notes, and eighth note triplets. Since this piece ends right handed, begin with your left hand when you repeat. Here is how the piece is counted.

1 & 2 &ah 3triplet 4 &. 1e& 2triplet 3e&ah 4 &. 1 &ah 2triplet 3e& 4triplet.
1e&ah 2 & 3triplet 4triplet. 1e&ah 2triplet 3triplet 4 &ah. 1triplet 2e& 3 &ah 4triplet.
1e& 2triplet 3e&ah 4 &. 1e& 2 &ah 3triplet 4e&ah. 1 &ah 2 &ah 3triplet 4e&ah.
1e&ah 2e& 3triplet 4triplet. 1 &ah 2triplet 3triplet 4e&. 1e& 2triplet 3e&ah 4 &ah.

NOTES:

Example 18

33

Example 19

Line 7: This is 12 measures long and combines eighth notes, eighth rests, eighth note triplets, and sixteenth notes. This is how the piece is counted:

1triplet 2 & 3e& 4triplet. 1 &ah 2triplet 3 & 4e&ah. 1 & 2triplet 3triplet 4 &ah.
1e&ah 2 & 3triplet 4e&. 1e& 2triplet 3 &ah 4triplet. 1 & 2triplet 3e&ah 4 &.
1 &ah 2e& 3triplet 4triplet. 1 & 2 & 3triplet 4 &ah. 1triplet 2 & 3e& 4triplet.
1triplet 2e&ah 3e& 4triplet. 1 & 2triplet 3e&ah 4triplet. 1 &ah 2e& 3triplet 4 &.

Line 8: This is 12 measures long and combines eighth notes, eighth rests, eighth note triplets, and sixteenth notes. This piece ends right handed, so begin with your left hand on the repeat. Here is how the piece is counted:

1triplet 2triplet 3 & 4e&. 1 &ah 2 & 3triplet 4triplet. 1e&ah 2triplet 3 &ah 4triplet.
1e&ah 2 & 3e& 4triplet. 1 &ah 2triplet 3e& 4triplet. 1triplet 2e&ah 3triplet 4 &.
1e& 2 & 3 &ah 4triplet. 1triplet 2e& 3 &ah 4triplet. 1e&ah 2 &ah 3triplet 4e&.
1 & 2triplet 3triplet 4 &ah. 1 &ah 2triplet 3e&ah 4 &ah. 1triplet 2triplet 3e&ah 4 &.

NOTES:

34

Example 19

35

Example 20

Line 9:   This is 12 measures long and combines eighth notes, eighth rests, eighth note triplets, sixteenth notes, and sixteenth rests. Make sure you count every note and rest written in order to keep steady time. Here is how the piece is counted.

> 1e&ah 2e&ah 3triplet 4 &. 1e&ah 2e&ah 3 & 4triplet. 1triplet 2e&ah 3 &ah 4triplet.
> 1e& 2triplet 3e&ah 4e&ah. 1e& 2triplet 3e&ah 4triplet. 1triplet 2e&ah 3 &ah 4e&ah.
> 1triplet 2triplet 3 &ah 4e&ah. 1 & 2e& 3 &ah 4triplet. 1e&ah 2triplet 3 & 4e&ah.
> 1e& 2triplet 3e&ah 4 &. 1triplet 2 &ah 3e& 4triplet. 1e& 2triplet 3 &ah 4e&ah.

Line 10: This is 12 measures long and combines eighth notes, eighth rests, eighth note triplets, sixteenth notes, and sixteenth rests. Since this piece ends right handed, begin with your left hand on the repeat. Here is how the piece is counted:

> 1 &ah 2triplet 3e&ah 4 &. 1 &ah 2triplet 3e&ah 4e&. 1e&ah 2 &ah 3e& 4triplet.
> 1triplet 2e& 3e&ah 4e&. 1e& 2e& 3triplet 4e&ah. 1triplet 2triplet 3e& 4 &ah.
> 1e&ah 2triplet 3triplet 4 &ah. 1e& 2e& 3triplet 4e&ah. 1 &ah 2e& 3triplet 4 &ah.
> 1e&ah 2triplet 3 &ah 4triplet. 1triplet 2e&ah 3e& 4 &. 1 &ah 2e&ah 3triplet 4 &.

NOTES:

Example 20

9

12 measures

10

12 measures

Example 21

Line 1 is comprised of two sixteenth note triplets. When two sixteenth note triplets are put together, they are referred to as a sextuplet. The definition of a sextuplet is - 6 notes played in the time of 4 notes. It really isn't any different than any other triplet. Why? The reason is simple. 6 notes played in the time of 4, and 3 notes played in the time of 2 amounts to the same thing. Each sixteenth note triplet in the phrase receives 1/2 beat. This is no different than the value of a sixteenth note triplet in 2/4 or 4/4 time.

Your foot goes down on 1, up on &, down an 2, up on &. Please take note that this is written in 2/4 time. These lines combine sextuplets, sixteenth note triplets, and eighth notes. Here is the counting for each line.

Line 1: 1triplet&triplet 2triplet&triplet

Line 2: Please notice the repeat measure - this is counted - 1triplet& 2triplet& for the first two measures.
    1 &triplet 2 &triplet for the last 2 measures.

Line 3: First two measures counted - 1triplet& 2 &triplet. Last two measures counted - 1 &triplet 2triplet&.

Line 4: 1 &triplet 2 &triplet (1st and 3rd measure). 1triplet& 2triplet& (2nd and 4th measures).

Line 5: First two measures counted - 1 &triplet 2triplet&. Last two measures counted - 1triplet& 2 &triplet.

Line 6: First two measures counted - 1triplet&triplet 2 &triplet. Last two measures counted - 1triplet&
    2triplet&triplet.

Line 7: First two measures counted - 1 &triplet 2triplet&triplet. Last two measures counted - 1triplet&triplet
    2triplet&.

Line 8: 1triplet& 2triplet&triplet. 1 &triplet 2triplet&triplet. 1triplet&triplet 2triplet&. 1triplet&triplet
    2 &triplet.

Line 9: This is 12 measures long and combines all of the previous rhythms. Here is how each measure is counted:

    1 &triplet 2triplet&. 1triplet& 2 &triplet. 1 &triplet 2triplet&triplet. 1triplet& 2triplet&.
    1 &triplet 2triplet&. 1 &triplet 2 &triplet. 1triplet&triplet 2triplet&. 1 &triplet 2triplet&triplet.
    1 &triplet 2triplet&. 1triplet& 2triplet&triplet. 1triplet&triplet 2 &triplet. 1triplet&triplet 2triplet&.

NOTES:

38

Example 21

39

Example 22

Line 10: This is 16 measures long and combines eighth notes, eighth note triplets, sixteenth note triplets, and sextuplets. Since this ends right handed, begin with your left hand on the repeat. Here is how this piece is counted.

1triplet 2triplet&. 1 &triplet 2triplet. 1triplet&triplet 2triplet. 1triplet 2 &triplet.
1triplet 2triplet&triplet. 1triplet& 2triplet. 1 &triplet 2triplet&triplet. 1triplet 2triplet&.
1triplet&triplet 2triplet&. 1triplet 2 &triplet. 1triplet& 2 &triplet. 1 &triplet 2triplet&.
1 &triplet 2triplet. 1triplet&triplet 2 &triplet. 1triplet 2triplet&. 1triplet 2 &triplet.

Line 11: This is 16 measures long and combines sextuplets, sixteenth note triplets, sixteenth notes, eighth note triplets, eighth notes, and eighth rests. Please take note of the 14th and 15th measures. Combined in these measures is a phrase of sixteenth notes and sixteenth note triplets. Here is how this piece is counted.

1triplet& 2 &triplet. 1 &triplet 2triplet. 1triplet& 2triplet&. 1triplet 2triplet&.
1 &ah 2triplet&. 1e& 2 &triplet. 1e&ah 2triplet. 1triplet&triplet 2 &.
1 &ah 2triplet&triplet. 1e& 2triplet&. 1triplet 2 &triplet. 1 &triplet 2 &.
1e& 2 &triplet. 1triplet&ah 2triplet. 1e&triplet 2triplet. 1 &triplet 2e&.

Line 12: This is 16 measures long and combines sextuplets, sixteenth note triplets, sixteenth notes, sixteenth rests, eighth note triplets, eighth notes, and eighth rests. Make sure you count every note and rest written in order to keep steady time. Here is how the piece is counted.

1triplet& 2 &ah. 1triplet 2triplet&triplet. 1e&ah 2e&ah. 1 &triplet 2e&.
1e&ah 2triplet&triplet. 1 &triplet 2e&ah. 1 &triplet 2triplet. 1e&ah 2triplet&.
1e&ah 2 &triplet. 1triplet&ah 2e&. 1triplet&triplet 2triplet. 1 &ah 2triplet&.
1 &triplet 2 &triplet. 1triplet& 2e&ah. 1triplet&triplet 2e&ah. 1triplet&triplet 2 &.

NOTES:

Example 22

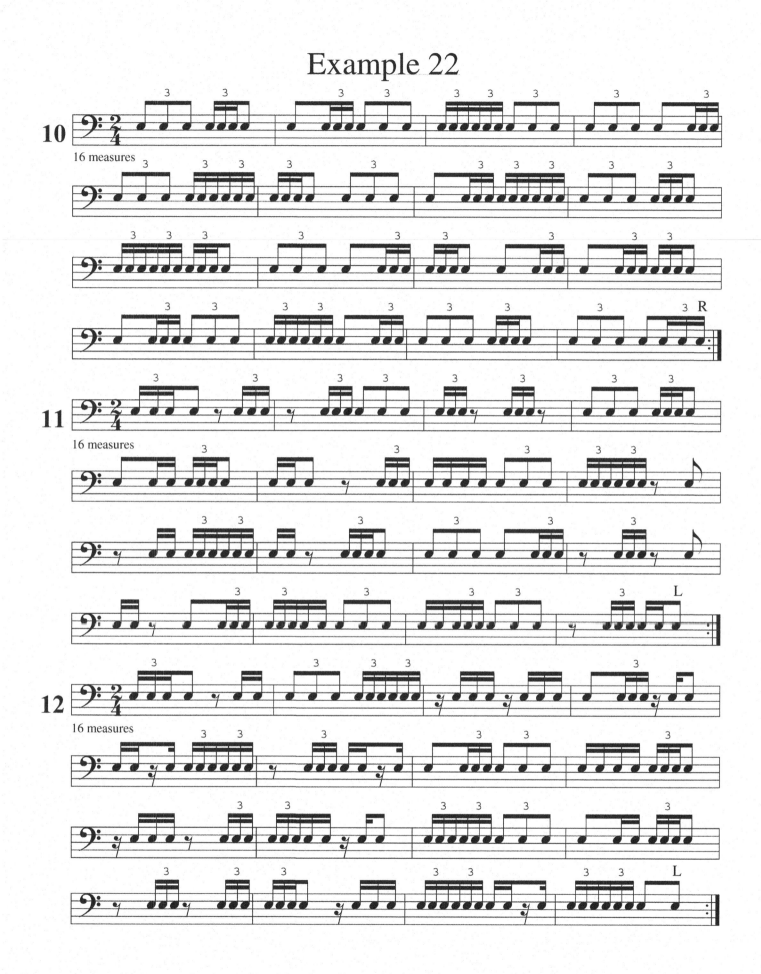

41

Example 23

Expression Marks. Learn all of your expression marks. Music begins to sound a little dull if it is played at the same volume all of the time. Expression marks give the music expression. Learn the letter for the expression mark, how to pronounce the word, and how it means to play. Let me give you a rule of thumb as to how to play these marks. The softer the volume, the closer your sticks should be to the drum. The louder the volume, the higher your sticks should be. Let the distance of the sticks help determine the volume.

pp   - Pianissimo - softer than piano. Pronounced "p-ah-niss-ah-mo".

mp   - Mezzo piano - medium soft.

p   - Piano - soft.

mf   - Mezzo forte - medium loud.

f   - Forte - loud. Pronounced "for-tay"

ff   - Fortissimo - louder than forte. Pronounced "for-tiss-ah-mo".

- Crescendo - gradually louder. Pronounced "cru-shen-doe".

- Diminuendo - gradually softer. Pronounced "d-min-u-en-doe"

Look over this piece and be aware of where the expression marks are. Please notice that there is a four measure introduction. Play to the end of the piece and repeat to the repeat sign (5th measure in the piece).

At this point, you should know how to count all of these measures. Concentrate on interpreting the expressive marks.

NOTES:

Example 23

Example 24

1st and 2nd endings: Here is how the 1st and 2nd endings work. Play the piece through the 1st ending. Repeat to the repeat sign (4th measure in the piece). Play the piece again, but, play the 2nd ending the second time through. In other words, play the 1st ending the first time through, play the 2nd ending the second time through. Follow all of the expression marks.

NOTES:

Example 24

Example 25

Dotted notes. Learn the definition of what a dot does to the note. A dot increases the note by 1/2 of the note's value.

A dotted half note ♩. is worth 3 beats.

A dotted quarter note ♩. is worth 1 1/2 beats.

A dotted eighth note ♪. is worth 3/4 of a beat.

Let's take a look at a few measures in this piece and explain how they are played and counted. In the 1st measure, there is a dotted half note and a quarter note. You strike the dotted half note on beat 1 and give the note 3 beats. You strike the quarter note on beat 4. You do not hit the dotted half note three times just because it gets 3 beats. Strike the note once. In the 3rd measure we have a dotted quarter note, eighth note, dotted quarter note, eighth note. Since the dotted quarter note gets 1 1/2 beats, give the dotted quarter note all of beat 1, and half of beat 2. The eighth note is then played on the & of 2. The next dotted quarter note is on beat 3. Give the dotted quartrer note all of beat 3, and half of beat 4. The eighth note is played on the & of 4. Let's stay with this dotted quarter note for just a moment. Look at the 9th measure. Here the dotted quarter note is on the & of 1, and the & of 3. It doesn't matter if the dotted quarter note is on the down stroke of the foot, or the up stroke of the foot. The dotted quarter note still gets 1 1/2 beats. The 9th measure is counted 1 & 2 3 & 4.

Take a look at the 4th measure. Beat 1 is a dotted eighth note followed by a sixteenth. The dotted eighth and the sixteenth is phrased like a sixteenth note, followed by two sixteenth rests, and a sixteenth note.

So this ♪. ♪ would be phrased like this: ♪ 𝄾 𝄾 ♪

Let me make something clear. If you play one note for 1e&, you have held the note for 3/4 of a beat. I wanted to make this distinction because I don't want you to think of dotted notes as being the same thing as a rest.

Now, let's count the 4th measure. The counting is - 1 ah 2 3 4 &. You play on the 1, ah of 1, beat 2, beat 3 and the & of 4. In the 13th measure, you see all dotted eighths followed by sixteenths. This measure is counted 1 ah 2 ah 3 ah 4 ah (3/4 of a beat followed by 1/4 of a beat).

It would be a good idea at this point to count the whold piece. The counting goes like this:

> 1 2 3 4. 1 2 3 4. 1 2 & 3 4 &. 1 ah 2 3 4 &.
> 1 2 & 3 ah 4 ah. 1 2 3 4 ah. 1 ah 2 3 ah 4.
> 1 2 3 4. 1 & 2 3 & 4. 1 & 2 & 3 ah 4.
> 1 ah 2 3 & 4. 1 2 3 4. 1 ah 2 ah 3 ah 4 ah.
> 1 2 & 3 4. 1 ah 2 3 ah 4. 1 ah 2 3 4.
> 1e&ah 2 ah 3 4 &. 1 & 2 ah 3e&ah 4. 1 & 2 3 & 4 ah.
> 1 2 & 3 & 4. 1 ah 2 ah 3 & 4. 1e&ah 2 & 3 ah 4.

Repeat to the beginning and play the piece one more time.

NOTES:

Example 25

Example 26

Line 1: *Ties*. A tie ties the notes together and makes them one note. Whatever the two notes add up to be in value, that's how long you hold the note. You play the note the tie is tied from, but do not play a separate note that the tie is tied to. In the 1st measure, a half note is tied to a half note. You play on beat 1, and hold the note for 4 beats. Two half notes tied together would be played like a whole note. In the 2nd measure, a half note is tied to a quarter note. You play on beat 1, and hold the note for 3 beats. You then play the quarter note on beat 4. In the 3rd measure, two quarter notes are tied together on beats 3 and 4. You play the quarter note on beat 3, and hold the note for beat 4. Two quarter notes tied together would be played like one half note. Let me give you an example of where tied notes come in very handy. Lets say we are on the 4th beat of a measure in 4/4 time. We need to play that note longer than 1 beat. What do you do? You tie beat 4 to a note written on beat 1 of the next measure. It would be wrong to write a measure of 5/4 or 6/4 time and change the feel of the piece of music you are playing. Therefore, you tie the note in order to hold the duration of the beat. Look over this piece and see where all of the ties occur and how long you should hold the note.

Line 2: In line 2 we have patterns of eighth notes and quarter notes. If a quarter note is tied to an eighth note, that note is worth 1 1/2 beats. If you tie two eighth notes together, it is played like a quarter note. Tying a 1/2 beat to a 1/2 beat gives us 1 beat. Look this piece over before you play it. See where all of the tied notes occur and how long you should hold the note.

NOTES:

Example 26

Example 27

The *sign* 𝄋, the *fine*, (pronounced "fee-nay") and the *fermata* 𝄐

When you see the sign 𝄋 you will also see the initials D.S. I will explain these terms. D.S. stands for Dal Segno which means go back to the Sign. Fine means the end.

A Fermata has two definitions. If the Fermata is over a note, you hold the note. If a Fermata is over a double bar, it means the end.

So, D.S. al Fine means go back to the Sign, and play to the end. So, here is how this piece works.

Play from the beginning to the end of the last line. Go back to the sign (beginning of the 5th line), and play to the Fine and Fermata (the 7th line, end of the 2nd bar). Once you have played from the Sign to the Fine, and the Fermata over the double bar, that is the end. You do not play the last four measures of the piece. Notes:

NOTES:

Example 27

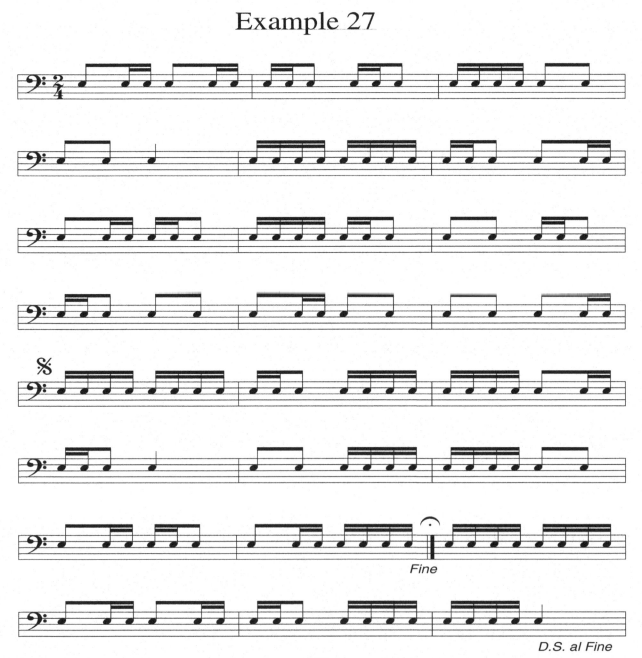

Fine

D.S. al Fine

Example 28

Coda ⊕

Da Capo, initialed D. C.

      D.C. al Coda means to go back to the beginning, play to the coda, skip to the next coda, and play to the end (Fine).

Here is how this piece works. Play from the beginning to the end of the 2nd measure of line 7. At this point you see the direction D.C. al Coda. Go back to the beginning and play to the first coda (beginning of the 3rd line). Skip to the next coda (last measure of the 7th line), and play to the end (Fine).Notes:

NOTES:

Example 28

D.C. al Coda

Fine

Example 29

Here are 8 measures using all of the notes and rhythms ranging from the whole note to the 32nd notes (I will explain how to play the 32nd notes). First, lets take a look at each measure. This starts with a whole note, goes to half notes, quarter notes, eighth notes, eighth note triplets, sixteenth notes, sextuplets, and 32nd notes. As you can see, the measures get progressively faster in hand speed. Start with a slow tempo. Keep the tempo the same throughout the 8 measures. Even though the tempo is slow, the sextuplets and 32nd notes will really fly by. If you start too fast, you may not be able to play the sextuplets and 32nd notes in steady time. Notice how there is a 6 above the sextuplets. They can be written with two 3's over them, or one 6. It does not change the way it is played. Now for the 32nd notes. 32nd notes are counted like sixteenth notes (1e&ah 2e&ah 3e&ah 4e&ah). The value for a 32nd note is 1/8th of a beat. So, instead of playing one note per syllable counted, you have to play two notes (4 notes when the foot is down, 4 notes when the foot is up). When you get to the end, repeat to the beginning. This way all of the notes and rhythms will have been played from hand to hand. Alternate each note after you have played two right hand strokes. Your whole note and your first half note should be right handed, the rest of the rhythmic patterns will be easier to play leading with your right hand.

NOTES:

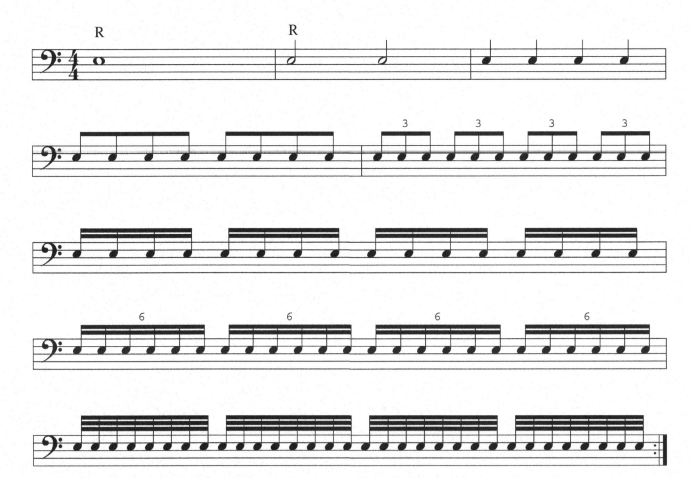